D1443135

TODAY'S ★ ★ ★ ★
AIR FORCE
HEROES

by Miriam Aronin

Consultant: Fred Pushies
U.S. SOF Adviser

BEARPORT
PUBLISHING

New York, New York

Credits

Cover and Title Page, © Image Source/SuperStock and U.S. Air Force/Capt. Tana Stevenson; 4, © Greg Martin/ SuperStock; 5, © U.S Air Force; 6, © U.S. Air Force/Staff Sgt James L. Harper Jr.; 7, © Ali Al-Saadi/AFP/Getty Images; 8T, © U.S. Air Force/Tech Sgt Jim Varhegyi; 8B, © Tony Linck/SuperStock; 9, © U.S. Marine Corps/ Cpl Jason Ingersoll; 10, © U.S. Air Force/Tech. Sgt. Jim Varhegyi; 11, © U.S. Air Force/Tech. Sgt. Jim Varhegyi; 12T, © U.S Air Force; 12B, © U.S Air Force; 13, © Check Six/Getty Images; 14, © U.S. Air Force/Staff Sgt. Shawn Weismiller; 15, © U.S. Air Force/Mr. Steve White; 16A, Courtesy of Lt. Col. Kim Campbell; 16B, © U.S. Air Force/Master Sgt. Robert Wieland; 17, © Alan Lessig/Air Force Times; 18, Courtesy of Lt. Col. Kim Campbell; 19, © Douglas R. Clifford/ZUMA Press/Newscom; 20T, © U.S. Air Force; 20B, © U.S. Army/Pvt. 1st Class Ali Hargis; 21, © U.S. Air Force/Airman 1st Class Devin Doskey; 22-23, © U.S. Air Force/Tech Sgt. Scott Reed; 23, © U.S. Air Force/Mr. Steve White; 24T, © U.S. Air Force; 24B, © U.S. Air Force/Staff Sgt. Adrian Cadiz; 25, © U.S. Air Force/Tech. Sgt. Shane Cuomo; 26, © U.S. Air Force; 27T, © U.S. Air Force/Staff Sgt. Shane A. Cuomo; 27B, © U.S. Air Force/Tech Sgt. Keith Brown; 28, © Mark Wilson/Getty Images; 29T, © U.S. Air Force/David W. Gilmore Jr.; 29B, © U.S. Air Force/Master Sgt. Keith Brown; 31, © Keith McIntyre/Shutterstock.

Publisher: Kenn Goin
Senior Editor: Lisa Wiseman
Creative Director: Spencer Brinker
Design: Dawn Beard Creative
Photo Researcher: Picture Perfect Professionals, LLC

Library of Congress Cataloging-in-Publication Data

Aronin, Miriam.
  Today's Air Force heroes / by Miriam Aronin ; consultant, Fred Pushies.
     p. cm. — (Acts of courage: inside America's military)
  Includes bibliographical references and index.
  Audience: Ages 7–12.
  ISBN-13: 978-1-61772-447-3 (library binding)
  ISBN-10: 1-61772-447-5 (library binding)
  1. United States. Air Force—Biography—Juvenile literature. 2. Airmen—United States—Juvenile literature. 3. Iraq War, 2003—Juvenile literature. 4. Afghan War, 2001—Juvenile literature. I. Pushies, Fred J., 1952– II. Title.
  UG633.A815 2012
  358.40092'273—dc23
                             2011039988

For more information, write to Bearport Publishing Company, Inc., 45 West 21st Street, Suite 3B, New York, New York 10010. Printed in the United States of America in North Mankato, Minnesota.

10 9 8 7 6 5 4 3 2 1

★★★ Contents ★★★

Attacked!

It was a beautiful, sunny morning on September 11, 2001, in New York City. At 8:46 A.M. firefighters in the station house of Ladder Company 6 heard a thunderous noise. When they rushed outside to see what was causing the sound, they were shocked. Above them an airplane was flying low—too low. Seconds later the plane crashed into the 110-story North Tower of the World Trade Center. Shortly after, a second plane crashed into the South Tower. It wasn't long before U.S. officials learned that the two planes had been **hijacked**.

Smoke poured from the towers after being attacked on September 11, 2001.

About two hours after being hit by the planes, both towers had collapsed.

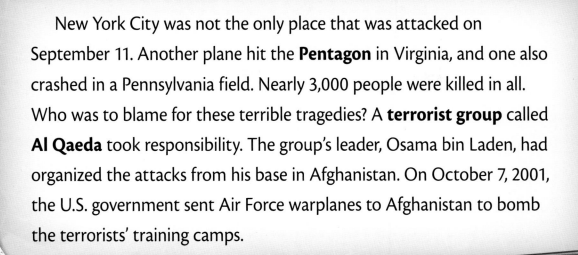

New York City was not the only place that was attacked on September 11. Another plane hit the **Pentagon** in Virginia, and one also crashed in a Pennsylvania field. Nearly 3,000 people were killed in all. Who was to blame for these terrible tragedies? A **terrorist group** called **Al Qaeda** took responsibility. The group's leader, Osama bin Laden, had organized the attacks from his base in Afghanistan. On October 7, 2001, the U.S. government sent Air Force warplanes to Afghanistan to bomb the terrorists' training camps.

Warplanes, such as this F-16, were sent to Afghanistan in October 2001.

War in Iraq

As the fight against terrorism continued, it expanded to Iraq. U.S. government officials believed that Saddam Hussein, the ruler of Iraq, was building powerful weapons, including **nuclear** ones, to use against the United States and other countries. They thought he needed to be stopped. As it had done in Afghanistan, the U.S. Air Force led the charge in Iraq with an air attack on March 20, 2003. Though weapons were never found, the U.S. and its **allies** were able to remove Saddam Hussein from power.

Members of the Air Force landing on a building rooftop in Iraq

The U.S. Air Force has served in many parts of Iraq and Afghanistan. The red parts on this map show where some of the events in this book took place.

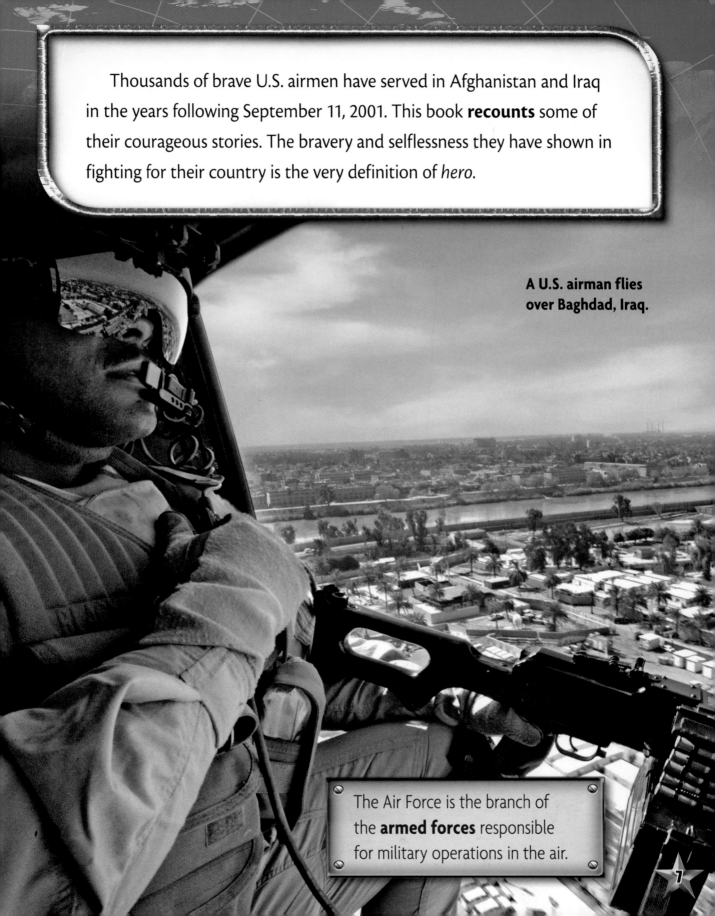

Thousands of brave U.S. airmen have served in Afghanistan and Iraq in the years following September 11, 2001. This book **recounts** some of their courageous stories. The bravery and selflessness they have shown in fighting for their country is the very definition of *hero*.

A U.S. airman flies over Baghdad, Iraq.

The Air Force is the branch of the **armed forces** responsible for military operations in the air.

"Is There Anybody in Here?"

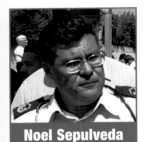
Noel Sepulveda

Rank:	Senior Master Sergeant
Born:	Puerto Rico
Conflict:	Al Qaeda attacks on the United States
Date:	September 11, 2001
Honor:	Airman's Medal and Purple Heart

On the morning of September 11, 2001, Senior Master Sergeant (Sgt.) Noel Sepulveda, a member of the Air Force **Reserve**, drove to the Pentagon for an important meeting. When he arrived, Pentagon workers told him that the building was being **evacuated**. Two planes had hit the World Trade Center in New York City. The Pentagon could be next. Senior Master Sgt. Sepulveda quickly ran outside.

The Pentagon is the headquarters of the U.S. military, including the U.S. Air Force.

When he reached the parking lot, he noticed a plane flying very low in the air—much lower than normal. A moment later, it crashed into the Pentagon. Part of the building exploded into flames. The impact of the explosion was so strong that it slammed Senior Master Sgt. Sepulveda into a light post, hurting his back and head.

Even though he was in pain, Senior Master Sgt. Sepulveda raced toward the burning building. If people were trapped inside, he had to help them. "Is everybody out? Is there anybody in here?" he shouted through a broken window.

A small section of the Pentagon was severely damaged by the crash.

Rescue at the Pentagon

Peering into one of the Pentagon's broken windows, Senior Master Sgt. Sepulveda could see a man staggering toward him. The man's hands and chest were badly burned. Senior Master Sgt. Sepulveda quickly climbed through the window to help him out of the building.

Within minutes, firefighters were at the scene, warning that the building might collapse at any time. Despite the danger and the intense heat from the fire, Senior Master Sgt. Sepulveda kept going back inside the smoke-filled building, working with other rescuers to help bring out more people.

Senior Master Sgt. Sepulveda (center) rescued people and organized emergency medical care at the Pentagon.

Senior Master Sgt. Sepulveda led the victims out of the chaos inside the building to a safe area. There, he helped organize a first aid station to care for the injured. By the end of the day, Senior Master Sgt. Sepulveda had helped at least eight people, including a two-month-old baby, get out of the burning building. For the next ten days, he continued to give medical treatment to the victims of the Pentagon attack.

On April 15, 2002, Noel Sepulveda (right) received the Airman's Medal as well as the Purple Heart for his heroic actions. He was the only person who received the Airman's Medal after the attack on the Pentagon.

The Airman's Medal is the highest U.S. award for **heroism** shown outside of combat situations. The Purple Heart is awarded to those who are wounded or killed while serving their country.

Courage Under Fire

Jason Cunningham

Rank: Senior Airman

Hometown: Carlsbad, New Mexico

Conflict: War in Afghanistan

Date: March 4, 2002

Honor: Air Force Cross

Like Senior Master Sgt. Sepulveda, Senior **Airman** Jason Cunningham always thought of others first. At sunrise on a bitterly cold day in March 2002, a helicopter carried Airman Cunningham and a team of **Army Rangers** toward a tall mountain in Paktia province, Afghanistan. They were on a mission to rescue a **Navy SEAL** who had fallen out of a helicopter when it was hit by rockets and gunfire from Al Qaeda forces.

Airman Cunningham (center) with two other airmen a few weeks before their mission in March 2002

As Airman Cunningham's chopper drew near the snowy mountaintop, Al Qaeda fighters attacked. Their powerful **rocket-propelled grenades** badly damaged the helicopter. Moments later, it crashed to the ground. Several soldiers were seriously injured. With the enemy fighters still shooting, the men couldn't be moved to a safe place. Airman Cunningham had no choice but to treat their wounds in the rear of the helicopter.

Airman Cunningham was a **pararescueman**. In Afghanistan, his job was to rescue those injured in battle and serve as a combat **medic**.

Airman Cunningham was in a helicopter, similar to this one, during his March 2002 mission.

Giving His Life

Along with another medic, Airman Cunningham worked on the soldiers while under constant enemy gunfire. Suddenly, the front of the helicopter caught on fire. They had to get out fast—before the deadly flames killed them.

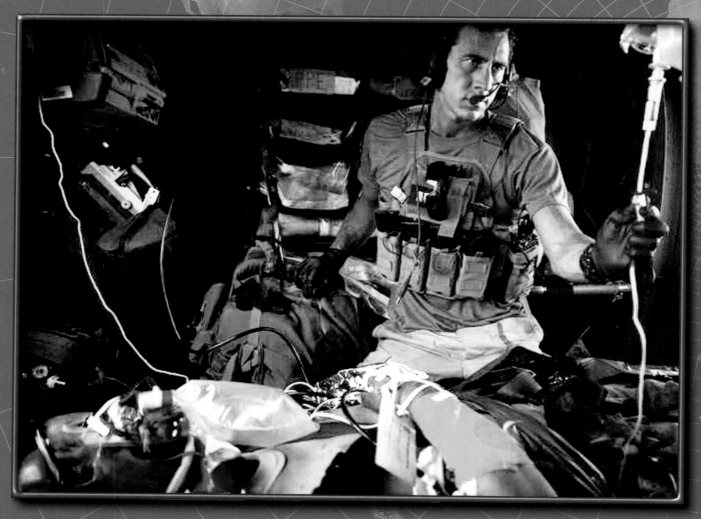

Like Airman Cunningham, this pararescueman gave medical treatment to a soldier on a helicopter.

Moving the men out of the helicopter to safety would be risky, but that didn't stop Airman Cunningham. Without hesitation, he dashed through the line of fire several times to carry wounded men away from the chopper. Even after an enemy bullet hit him on the side, he refused to stop treating the wounded. After seven hours, however, Airman Cunningham had lost so much blood that he couldn't keep helping the others. He died surrounded by his fellow soldiers on the cold mountainside in Afghanistan— where that day he'd helped save ten lives.

Air Force Cross

Airman Cunningham was laid to rest in Arlington National Cemetery in Virginia. This has been the U.S. national military cemetery since 1864.

In September 2002, in front of about 1,400 people, Jason Cunningham's wife and his parents accepted the Air Force Cross for his heroic actions in combat. This medal is the second-highest honor awarded to a member of the U.S. Air Force. Here, Jason's fellow pararescuemen gather at a ceremony in his honor.

The Warthog Is Hit

Kim Campbell

Rank:	Captain (Promoted to Major in 2010)
Hometown:	San Jose, California
Conflict:	Iraq War
Date:	April 7, 2003
Honor:	Distinguished Flying Cross

The year after Jason Cunningham's last mission in Afghanistan, the United States went to war in Iraq. A few weeks into the war, American soldiers found themselves under heavy attack in Baghdad, the Iraqi capital. To help them, the Air Force's 23rd Fighter Group flew to Baghdad, 300 miles (483 km) from its base in Kuwait. From the air, fighter pilots, including Captain (Capt.) Kim Campbell, fired powerful guns and missiles on the Iraqi troops below.

Capt. Campbell flew a type of plane nicknamed the "Warthog." Its official name is the A-10 Thunderbolt II.

During the mission, Capt. Campbell felt enemy fire hit her plane. Warning lights flashed inside. They showed that the **hydraulic system** that controlled the steering was no longer working. Would Capt. Campbell be able to fly the damaged Warthog back to base without crashing?

The enemy fire that hit Capt. Campbell's plane left hundreds of holes in it.

In 2003, there were fewer than 50 female fighter pilots in the U.S. Air Force.

Back to Base

With the hydraulic system down, Capt. Campbell was under a lot of pressure, but she remained cool. She quickly switched to the **manual** controls. She would now have to fly the plane without the help of its hydraulic system—not an easy task. To get back safely, Capt. Campbell had to work extra hard and stay very alert. Otherwise, her plane could easily crash in enemy territory, where she could be hurt or captured. "The trip back . . . was one of the longest hours of my life," she said.

Very few pilots have successfully used manual controls to land a damaged Warthog. Some who tried were either injured or killed.

Lieutenant Colonel Richard Turner (right) was on the same mission as Capt. Campbell and helped guide her back to base from his plane.

At last the base was in sight. As Capt. Campbell approached, she felt she could make the difficult landing perfectly, and she did. "It was an amazing feeling of relief," she said.

In the days and weeks after her frightening brush with disaster, Capt. Campbell kept flying, helping U.S. troops in Iraq. In fact, she flew another mission in a new Warthog the very day after her brave flight back from Baghdad.

Distinguished
Flying Cross

Directing Jets

Earl Covel

Rank: Staff Sergeant
Hometown: Oregon City, Oregon
Conflict: Iraq War
Date: June 18, 2004
Honor: Silver Star

Staff Sgt. Earl Covel also became an Air Force hero while serving in Iraq. On June 18, 2004, he sent out an urgent call for help on his radio. A group of about 200 **insurgents** was attacking the building where his 18-man team was hiding. His team could not hold off the enemy fighters for long.

About half of Sgt. Covel's team was made up of **Kurds**. Many Kurdish fighters had opposed the Iraqi government for a long time. So when the war began, they fought alongside American forces.

Kurdish fighters called *peshmerga* helped the Americans.

U.S. fighter jets were sent to join the battle. However, the pilots needed to know which targets to bomb and when to attack. Sgt. Covel could direct them by radio, but only if he could see the area clearly. The best view was from the roof of the building next door. From there, he could see everything. However, if he went up on the roof, the enemy could see him, too.

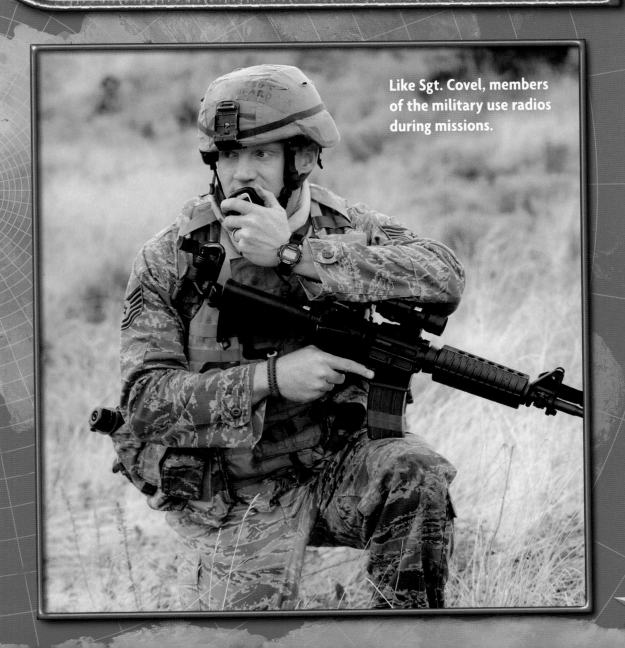

Like Sgt. Covel, members of the military use radios during missions.

Danger on the Rooftop

Without hesitation, Sgt. Covel went up to the rooftop of the other building. As soon as he got there, insurgents fired at him. They shot at him again and again while he shot back with his rifle. Fortunately, he was not hit.

Despite the danger, Sgt. Covel stayed on the roof, directing the fighter jets by radio. He did not leave his post until the fighting ended 36 hours later.

During the mission in 2004, Sgt. Covel directed powerful fighter planes called F-18s. These planes can strike targets on the ground and also fight other aircraft in the air.

Sgt. Covel's bravery helped the Americans win the battle and kept all his team members safe. The soldiers were so grateful that they recommended him for the Silver Star—an award given for heroism while risking one's life.

The Silver Star

On May 11, 2007, Sgt. Covel was awarded the Silver Star. It is the third-highest combat medal awarded for bravery while facing an enemy.

"Definitely Danger"

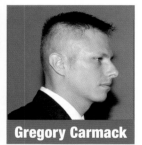

Gregory Carmack

Rank:	Special Agent
Home State:	North Carolina
Conflict:	Iraq War
Date:	June 14, 2006
Honor:	Bronze Star with Valor

On June 14, 2006, Air Force Special Agent Gregory Carmack and nine other special agents met up with an Army Humvee **convoy** in Kirkuk, a city in Iraq. They were all working together on a mission to capture two dangerous terrorists.

Humvees, as shown here, are large jeep-like military vehicles.

Humvees are not only used to take members of the military on missions. They are used to carry supplies, and often serve as ambulances, too.

Suddenly, a white pickup truck ran over an Iraqi policeman as it sped toward Agent Carmack and the others. Agent Carmack realized right away that everyone was in danger. "It was most likely a **suicide bomber**," he said. The special agent knew he had to act fast to save lives. Seconds later, he shot the driver.

Agent Carmack (right) was in Iraq to help gather information about the enemy.

"Heroes in Our Ranks"

Bomb experts later found powerful explosives hidden under the truck's passenger seat. Thanks to Agent Carmack's quick thinking, the driver had not had a chance to **detonate** them. The special agent's heroic actions had saved the lives of the American soldiers.

On September 13, 2007, Agent Gregory Carmack received the Bronze Star with Valor. It is the fourth-highest combat award given by the U.S. Armed Forces.

Air Force heroes like Agent Carmack risk their lives every day for their country. Their **sacrifices** help protect Americans and people around the world. In the words of Secretary of the U.S. Air Force Michael Donley, "We are blessed as a nation, as an Air Force, to have so many heroes in our ranks."

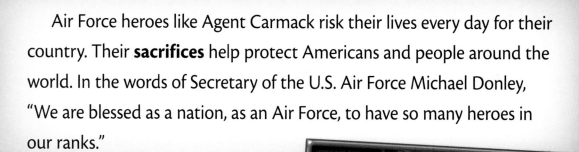

In 2010, more than 330,000 Americans were serving in the U.S. Air Force.

More Air Force Heroes

Here are a few members of the U.S. Air Force who have performed heroic acts away from combat.

⭐ Master Sergeant John W. Jackson ⭐

After Hurricane Katrina hit the Mississippi coast in 2005, Air Force Master Sgt. John W. Jackson, who lived in Biloxi, Mississippi, sprang into action. He raised money to help people whose homes and belongings were destroyed in the storm. He even invited an elderly neighbor, who had lost her home in the hurricane, to share his family's home. The next year, Master Sgt. Jackson was honored in a ceremony for his heroic service to others.

Hurricane Katrina hit the Mississippi coast in 2005.

⭐ Chief Master Sergeant John Gebhardt ⭐

In September 2006, Air Force Chief Master Sgt. John Gebhardt was helping out at his base hospital in Iraq. One of the patients was a young, injured Iraqi girl whose entire family had been killed by insurgents. Often, when the injured child could not sleep well, Chief Master Sgt. Gebhardt helped her stay calm by holding her. His attention to the young girl helped ease the pain of her difficult recovery.

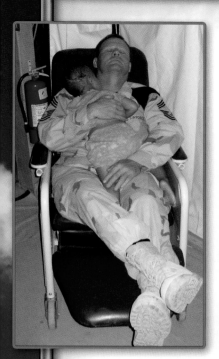

Chief Master Sgt. Gebhardt holds the young girl as they both sleep.

⭐ Lieutenant Colonel (Dr.) Thomas Knolmayer ⭐

In 2008, Air Force Lieutenant Colonel (Dr.) Thomas Knolmayer, who was stationed at a hospital in Afghanistan, asked his wife to send him some of their son's old hiking boots. He wanted to give them to one of his patients, a five-year-old boy who had no shoes. When Mrs. Knolmayer told her friends about her husband's request, they sent shoes and clothing, too. The doctor collected enough shoes and clothes for hundreds of Afghan children.

Lieutenant Colonel (Dr.) Knolmayer helps an Afghan girl try on a pair of donated shoes.

Glossary

airman (AIR-man) the first rank for enlisted men and women after completing Air Force basic training

allies (AL-eyez) friends or supporters

Al Qaeda (AHL KAY-duh) the terrorist group that was responsible for the September 11, 2001, attacks on the United States

armed forces (ARMD FORSS-iz) the military groups a country uses to protect itself; in the United States these are the Army, the Navy, the Air Force, the Marines, and the Coast Guard

Army Rangers (AR-mee RAYN-jurz) members of the U.S. Army who have been specially trained for difficult missions

convoy (KON-voi) a group of military vehicles traveling together for safety

detonate (DET-uh-*nate*) to cause something to explode

evacuated (i-VAK-yoo-*ate*-id) moved people away from an area because it is dangerous

heroism (HAIR-oh-*iz*-uhm) bravery

hijacked (HYE-jackt) illegally took control of an airplane or other vehicle by force

hydraulic system (hye-DRAW-lik SISS-tuhm) a system that works from power created by liquid being forced under pressure through pipes

insurgents (in-SUR-junts) people who fight against a lawful government or leaders

Kurds (KURDZ) a group of people who live in parts of Armenia, Iran, Iraq, Syria, and Turkey

manual (MAN-yoo-uhl) worked by hand, not by machine

medic (MED-ik) a person trained to give medical care

Navy SEAL (NAY-vee SEEL) a sailor in the U.S. Navy who is specially trained to fight at sea, in the air, and on land

nuclear (NOO-klee-ur) having to do with a dangerous type of energy that produces radiation

pararescueman (*pah*-ruh-RESS-kyoo-man) an airman who is trained to make rescues, give medical care, and fight in combat

Pentagon (PEN-tuh-gon) the five-sided building in Virginia that serves as the headquarters of the U.S. Department of Defense

rocket-propelled grenades (ROK-it-pruh-PELD gruh-NAYDS) weapons often used by insurgents to damage or destroy buildings or vehicles

recounts (ri-COUNTS) tells about something in detail

reserve (ri-ZURV) part of the U.S. military made up of people who are called in to help during emergencies, or in time of war

sacrifices (SAK-ruh-*fysess*-iz) things people give up for important reasons

suicide bomber (SOO-uh-*side* BOM-ur) a person who carries out an attack by blowing up a bomb attached to his or her body

terrorist group (TER-ur-ist GROOP) people who use violence and threats to get what they want

Bibliography

Larlee, Staff Sgt. Jeremy. "Humble Chief Gains National Attention." *Air Force Print News* (November 10, 2006). http://www.af.mil/news/story.asp?id=123031670

Sherman, Patrick. "Hometown Hero." *The Clackamas Review* (May 16, 2007). www.clackamasreview.com/news/story.php?story_id=117918147658885100

Vadnais, Tech. Sgt. Chris. "Special Agent Proves Airmen Are 'In The Fight.'" Air Force News Agency (October 4, 2007). http://www.af.mil/news/story.asp?id=123070654

ourmilitaryheroes.defense.gov/

Read More

Goldish, Meish. *Air Force: Civilian to Airman (Becoming a Soldier).* New York: Bearport Publishing (2011).

Hamilton, John. *The Air Force (Defending the Nation).* Edina, MN: Checkerboard (2007).

Sandler, Michael. *Pararescuemen in Action (Special Ops).* New York: Bearport Publishing (2008).

Learn More Online

To learn more about today's U.S. Air Force heroes, visit
www.bearportpublishing.com/ActsofCourage

Index

About the Author

Miriam Aronin is a writer and editor. She also enjoys reading, dancing, and knitting. She would like to dedicate this book to her cousins Chaya, Yossi, Michoel, Necha, Menucha, and Moss.